BMW

BMW

COLOUR, DATA AND DETAIL ON
FOUR DECADES OF
BMW CARS

**Martin Buckley
and James Mann**

Windrow & Greene Automotive

Published in Great Britain by
Windrow & Greene Ltd
5 Gerrard Street
London W1V 7LJ

A C.I.P. catalogue record for this book is available from the British Library.

ISBN 1 872004 13 X

Designed by: *ghk* DESIGN, Chiswick, London

Printed in Singapore

Contents

Acknowledgements

Thanks first of all to BMW GB in Bracknell for access to their historic car collection (328, M6, M1, 507 and Z1). Thanks also to Chris Willows of BMW Public Relations for the loan of pictures from his own personal collection, and to the BMW historic archives in Munich for the loan of some excellent colour and black-and-white pictures. All other shots are originals by James Mann. Finally, thanks to my publishers, Windrow & Greene Automotive, for the opportunity to write a book on a subject close to my heart!

Martin Buckley
London, July 1993

Introduction

Not until six years after hostilities had drawn to a close was BMW able to introduce the first of its postwar cars. The 501, shown to the public at the 1951 *Internationale Automobil-Ausstellung*, was far from being the greatest car ever to wear the famous blue roundel. It was a paunchy overweight saloon with a hard-pushed two-litre 326 engine, but that it appeared at all was a minor miracle for the Munich company.

Because of the company's war-time 'plane-building activities, punitive allied action had made BMW's recovery even harder than it would normally have been. Furthermore, to compound their difficulties the Eisenach car-plant was in East Germany, occupied now of course by the Russians. By building BMW-badged pre-war models they only added to the Munichers' misery, and it was not until 1952 that they were finally compelled to drop the trademark. From then, until Wartburg production began in the mid-1950s, the cars (still '30s machines mutilated by Detroit-style front ends) were grudgingly dubbed EMWs, with the blue segments of the badge changed to red.

Above: Ancestor. Beautiful, technically refined and a superb driver's car, the 328 was one of the finest all-round sports cars available in the 1930s. Production lasted from 1936 to 1940, totalling 459.

Below: Bulbous 502 V8 was BMW's immediate postwar staple. A fine, fast car, it was too expensive to sell in significant numbers.

More than 10 years were to pass before BMW's real renaissance began. Following the resumption of motorcycle production in 1948 — which was hit, in any case, by the number of small economy cars coming on to the market — they scraped through the 1950s building the big 501 saloon, joined by a much better V8 version in 1954, and a pair of big-money sportscars, the 503 and 507, neither of which brought in sufficient buyers. Both models are deserving of the epithet 'classic', however. The 507 had a purity of line rarely seen outside the great Italian styling houses and a turn of speed which only the Mercedes 300SL could equal on German roads — as much as 135mph with the longest axle ratio option. The 503 came as a closed coupé or a pretty convertible, using the tuned 507 engine with the saloon-length wheelbase. Count Albrecht Goertz, a German-American design consultant, designed both cars.

The last car to use this forgotten alloy V8 was the elegant Bertone-designed 3200CS of 1962 — a styling pointer to the mass-produced BMW coupés yet to come.

Below: The 507. Fast, exquisitely styled and very expensive, it used a separate chassis, alloy bodywork and a tuned version of BMW's aluminium V8 engine.

Inevitably BMW was plagued by financial troubles during these years (Mercedes were potential buyers when bankruptcy threatened, as late as 1959), but the Isetta bubble and later the 700 range helped keep its corporate head above water. The Isetta was based on a design by ISO of Italy (later supercar builders) and came with three or four wheels and a single front door hinged on the left. Power came from a single-cylinder 247/297cc engine giving 12-13 bhp for a top speed of 53mph. In 1957 BMW developed their own four-seat alternative, the 600, with four wheels only, one side door to supplement the front opening, and a bigger 582cc twin. Over 200,000 of all these baby BMWs were built, and it was perhaps fortunate for the company's image that the public at large never regarded them as 'proper' BMWs.

Styled by Michelotti and looking rather like a cleaned-up Triumph Herald, the 700 was a conventionally-proportioned saloon with a rear-mounted two-cylinder engine. It came as both coupé and convertible and sold strongly right up to its demise in 1965.

It was in 1961 that BMW was able to announce the truly modern saloon car that German's burgeoning middle-classes really wanted.

The 1500 *Neue Klasse* struggled into production in 1962, since when BMW has scarcely looked back. Crisply styled, intelligently engineered and enjoyable to drive in a way the lumbering sixes and V8s could never be, the 1500 spawned a whole generation of four-cylinder saloons (and a glamorous coupé) which achieved strong sales well into the 1970s and established BMW as a major European manufacturer. The engineering basics survive to this day: in-line SOHC engine, MacPherson strut front suspension, semi-trailing arms at the back and a strong unitary shell — modern, glassy, but without pretension.

The merits of the 1500 were noted by America's influential *Car and Driver* magazine, whose comments virtually summarised the philosophy on which BMW's reputation was to be founded: 'in addition to the remarkably careful design work and the good technical solutions… both choice of materials and assembly methods were on a par with the best in the German auto industry'.

The range developed quickly, from the 80bhp 92mph 1500 in 1962 to a 100mph 1800 in 1963, a 1600 in 1964, and a two-litre car in 1966. Later the 1600-2/2002 — the same engineering in a two-door body — defined the hot small car and established BMW in the all-important American market. Kugelfischer developed a mechanical injection system for the four-cylinder engine, boosting its output to 130bhp (for the Tii cars), and much later in 1973 there appeared the controversial 2002 Turbo, launched in the midst of an energy crisis: it was fast, violently accelerative and had massive boy-racer appeal, but was the wrong car for those cautious times. It lasted a year and only 1,672 were built.

In 1968 BMW re-entered the big car market with the six-cylinder saloons and coupés,

Above: 1600-2 (later 1602) was a huge success for BMW, a cheaper two-door car with fine handling which survived into the mid-1970s as a bargain entry-level model.

Below: Ultimate 02 car was the Turbo of 1973. Violently fast, garishly trimmed, it was not the right car for the fuel-crisis years. It lasted only until 1974 and is now highly collectable.

every bit as class-leading as the epoch-making 1500 of seven years before. Refined but sporting, with a fine new engine, BMW had grown up together with Germany's increasingly affluent society, whose members were now forsaking the stark efficiency of the four-cylinder New Class cars for the sumptuous luxury of these new Mercedes challengers. Engines grew to 3.3 litres in the early 1970s and the wheelbase was stretched to rival Mercedes' big SEL S-Class cars, but the big BMWs always had a more sporting, youthful appeal.

The six-cylinder CS coupés were styling classics, their quali-

Above: The big six-cylinder saloons re-established BMW in the luxury car market. Built as 2500, 2800, 3.0 and 3.3-litre versions, they remained in production from 1968 to 1977. This is a long-wheelbase 3.0 L.

ties as valid today as when they were first introduced. Based on the 2000CS centre section and tail, but with new front-end styling to match the big saloons, the 2800 three-litre coupés were the most popular cars in the luxury coupé class for years. Injection was added later, plus a charismatic lightweight homologation special, the CSL, with lightweight alloy opening panels. Factory and privately entered CSL coupés won the Group 2 ETC five times, their success continuing three years after the road cars went out of production. Bodies were built by Karmann (famous for his special-bodied VWs) and production ended in 1975.

In the 1970s, expansion not only continued but gained momentum. New Class gave way to 5-Series, the new small two-door BMWs became 3-Series, and by the end of the decade the six-cylinder saloon and coupé had become 6- and 7-Series cars — none of them radically different in engineering, but simply subtle and intelligent refinements of what the Munich engineers knew to be both saleable and 'right'. They were still very much drivers' cars, though now somewhat softened for a market which required more and more luxury and refinement. In fact, the 6-Series in particular was not quite the nimble car the old coupé had been, though it was given a fillip in the mid-1980s when BMW's motorsport division stuffed the twin-cam M1 engine into the nose to create the now sorely-missed M635 CSi.

The M1 itself was a curious diversion for the company — yet another homologation car for Group 4 racing, partly developed by Lamborghini during the late 1970s before the company ran into

Below: The six-cylinder coupés were classically elegant and among the most successful cars in their class despite high prices. Shown is the 3.0 CS.

financial difficulties. It was a mid-engined fibreglass supercar, styled by Ital Design and powered by a 277bhp twin-cam six developed from the racing CSL engines. 397 were built and the car achieved only limited race-track success.

There were hot 'M' versions of the 5-Series as well — sure to be collectable some day — and even a Turbo version of the 7-Series to make up for BMW's lack of a V12 engine to use in their flagship saloon. 3-Series devotees had to wait for the second-generation range before getting their M car, but it was worth the wait: here was a thinly-disguised homologation street racer of rare ability, using a unique twin-cam four-cylinder 200bhp engine for 150mph maximum speed, shattering acceleration and truly inspired handling. This car, and the M3 Evolution which followed, are headed straight for collectable status.

In Britain, where the BMW name had been familiar only to fast car buffs and motorcycle enthusiasts, it was by now a symbol of German engineering solidity every bit as potent as Mercedes — with the bonus of a sporting image which the stuffier Stuttgart product lacked.

Now yet another generation of BMWs is with us: still rear-driven with their engines mounted up front, still beautifully built and still drivers' cars, even if the men and women who buy them are sometimes more interested in the go-getting, upwardly mobile image they project than in the performance and pleasure they offer. The 1990 3-Series, with its rounded, stand-alone styling, has caused a sensation, earning extravagant praise for its impeccable chassis manners, refinement and performance. The coupé version is the prettiest BMW for a long time, while in the executive class there is still little to equal the latest 5-Series, especially now that the top-of-the-range models are served by new multi-valve three- and four-litre V8s of rare smoothness.

The classic six survives, just, in the M5, which with the latest suspension tweaks and searing straight-line muscle is widely regarded as the best all-round saloon available.

At the top of the range, customers can now buy their BMW in V12

Above: The 3-Series replaced the 02 cars as the small BMWs in 1975 and came later with a new, smaller six-cylinder engine. Hottest of the range was the 323i.

Below: From 1982 there was a new 3-Series with cleaner styling, more cabin space and much-improved roadholding.

form, either in the big 7-Series (coming to the end of its days as this is written but still perhaps the most nimble of the European luxury cars), or in the 850 coupé — though this latter model has not succeeded in winning the hearts of BMW enthusiasts. For all its technical sophistication and undeniable competence, the car lacks charm, somehow, and its massive five-litre V12 provides neither the punch nor, more importantly, the smooth-ness which one would expect, especially in automatic form. A new bigger-engined version has hopefully cured the coupé's ills, but the company is clearly disillusioned with the car and, according to rumour, will not be replacing it. A cheaper four-litre V8 version is expected to bolster sales.

Above: 1989 M3 Evolution. Only 500 of these 220bhp supercars were built.

Below: The 850i was BMW's prestige V12 coupé for the 1990s — a fine open-road express, but in some people's view too big and too refined to have genuine driver-appeal.

Big car woes apart (and most other prestige manufacturers have those in the early 1990s), BMW's position is as strong as it ever was. No-one need doubt that some of the world's greatest drivers' cars, both large and small, will still be wearing that unmistakeable blue roundel in the next century.

BMW Postwar Production Chronology

1950 501 saloon introduced; enters production in 1951.

1955 V8-engined 502 saloon announced. Three-wheel Isetta bubble car starts production.

1956 503 coupé convertible and 507 roadster announced.

1958 600 joins Isetta with four seats and four wheels plus innovative semi-trailing arm rear suspension, but retains flat twin bike engine.

1960 700 announced: available in saloon, coupé and convertible versions.

1961 1500 'New Class' saloon announced. Later joined by 1800 version, some with twin carbs.
3200 CS announced, using last of the V8 chassis with Bertone bodywork.

1965 Karmann-bodied 2000 C/CS announced, using New Class engineering.

1966 1600-2 announced: a lower-priced two-door car using New Class engineering.

1968 Six-cylinder saloons — 2500/2800 — enter production. Also 2800 CS coupé, based on 2000 CS with with new front-end styling. Two-litre engine in 1600-2 chassis produces 2002.

1971 Kugelfischer injected 2002 Tii announced, plus three-litre versions of big saloons and coupés with carbs and optional Bosch injection. Also lightweight CSL with alloy bonnet, doors and bootlid for racing homologation.

1972 5-Series replaces New Class range, initially with four-cylinder 1.8 and two-litre engines.

1973 2002 Turbo announced, with 170bhp turbocharged engine, spoilers and Turbo badging; dies a year later. Also long wheelbase L saloons announced as top-of-the-range cars with Batmobile CSL and 525/528 six-cylinder 5-Series cars.

1975 New 3-Series replaces 02 cars: 316 and 320/320i versions.

1976 6-Series 630 and 633 CSi coupés replace 3.0CSi/CSa.

1977 7-Series replaces 2500/three-litre saloons as top-of-the-range cars. New small six in 3- and 5-Series.

1978 635i replaces 633 CSi; 628 replaces 630 from 1979.

1979 M1 production begins (ends 1980).

1980 745i introduced (produced in lhd form only).

1981 5-Series improved with new nose styling.

1982 New 3-Series announced with improved suspension, new styling and more space: 316, 320 and 323i versions. 7-Series improved with new 732i version and top-line 735i.

1985 M653 CSi introduced with 3.5-litre twin-cam engine. 325i joins 3-Series range, replacing 323i.

1986 Z1 enters production (continues to 1991).

1988 New 5-Series introduced

1991 New 3-Series and 850i coupé introduced.

1992 Two-door 3-Series and 5-Series Touring Estate debut.

1993 Convertible version of new 3-Series introduced.

1993 840CSi and 850CSi introduced.

1994 New 'Compact' 316i launched in Germany in the spring.

Postwar Confusion

From Baroque Angel to 3200CS

BAROQUE ANGELS — BMW struggled into production with the 501 saloon in 1952, using the old 326 1971cc, 65bhp engine in a new box section chassis. It was refined, but grossly underpowered. The V8 cars — using the same shell, but with a 2.6-litre alloy V8 — were far superior but were still too big and expensive to enjoy much popular appeal. The shape was nicknamed 'Baroque Angel' because of its resemblance to the chubby horn-blowing figures adorning baroque-period architecture. Still, the cars sold steadily to the German middle classes and provided a basis for some fine sporting machinery — the 503, 507 and 3200CS.

Opposite page

Top: The Baroque Angel saloons do have a certain bulbous elegance. The cars ran from 1952 to 1963 and were constantly improved. Six-cylinder models grew in capacity to become the 2077cc, 72bhp 501/3 capable of 90mph. Gearbox was positioned under front seats on early cars.

Below: This is a 502, with the alloy pushrod V8 pushing out 100bhp for a near 100mph top speed. Foglights in the wings and a chrome waist trim differentiated it from the 501. This post-September 1955 model also has the wrap-around rear window. There was also a 'bog-standard' V8 known as the 501 V8 from April 1955 (without extra trim and foglights), and a bigger 3.2-litre-engined V8 with 120bhp and 105mph potential known as the 3.2, which from 1960 on could be had with disc brakes and even power steering. From 1957, a 140bhp 3.2 Super was added. The standard V8 became known as the 2.6 in 1958 and from late 1961 as the 2600 (or slightly higher-powered 2600L). Final variation was the 3200/3200S, the latter's twin Zenith-fed 160bhp version of the engine making it Germany's fastest saloon at the time with a top speed of 118mph.

Above: Period advertisement for the big saloon — a 502, in this case. The high prices of the cars restricted their sales both in Germany and abroad.

Below: This 505 Pullman limousine was built in 1955 on a stretched 502 chassis, to compete with Mercedes in the 'state limo' stakes. Built by Ghia Aigle in Switzerland, its career as an official carriage was ended when Chancellor Konrad Adenauer knocked off his hat climbing into it! Only two were built, one of them retained by the factory where it survives among the BMW Oldtimer collection.

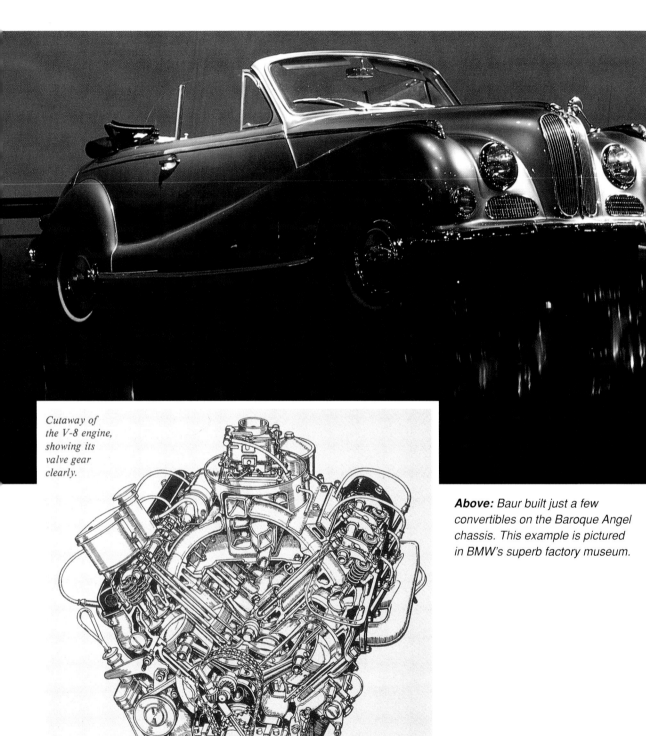

Cutaway of the V-8 engine, showing its valve gear clearly.

Above: *Baur built just a few convertibles on the Baroque Angel chassis. This example is pictured in BMW's superb factory museum.*

Left: *Big V8 was first mass production unit to use alloy block and head. Power went from 95bhp for 501 V8 to 160bhp in 3200S cars with twin Zenith carbs. Rumour has it that BMW sold the design to Buick.*

Below: The 503 cabrio, first seen at the Frankfurt Show in 1955: a superbly proportioned open car with classic long bonnet, long boot, short passenger compartment dimensions. Bodies were built in light alloy, although they always weighed as much as the saloons — a portly 3300lbs. The V8 in twin-carb, 140bhp 'S' form provided 118mph at the top end with 0-60mph attainable in 13 seconds — excellent for the time. This car has standard bolt-on wheels, but 507-style knock-on items were an extra cost option.

CIVILISED PERFORMERS: 503, 507 AND 3200CS — To broaden the appeal of their V8 range, BMW introduced the 503 in 1956. Styled by Albrecht Goertz, the cars came as a 2+2 coupé or convertible, with same-length chassis (111.6in wheelbase) and 140bhp 3200S V8 engine. More dramatic was the 507, a Mercedes 300SL-challenger on a shorter wheelbase than the 503, but with a superbly elegant two-seater roadster body, an all-time classic again styled by Goertz. Neither were all-out supercars: they would be better described as fast, expensive touring machines. The 3200CS was a meeting of '60s GT coupé styling — establishing a look which can still be recognised today in the latest 850i — and '50s engineering. Bodies were designed and built in Italy by Bertone and the car was an undeniably stylish way of getting rid of the final 3200S saloon chassis.

Above: If anything, the coupé was even more elegant, its extravagant lines possessing an almost pre-war grandeur. Its price of DM30,000 was DM12,000 higher than the mechanically identical 3.2 saloon. Later versions had disc brakes all round and a centrally mounted floor gearlever; pre-September 1957 cars needed column shift thanks to underseat gearbox mounting.

Left: Interiors were lavishly trimmed, with standard power windows among the luxury items.

Above: *Announced at the 1955 Paris Show and going into production the following year, the 507 is probably the most sought-after postwar BMW — a real classic-from-birth car whose Goertz styling has near-flawless balance. Built with American sales in mind (US importer Max Hoffman had a hand in its creation), it was more long-legged tourer than 300SL challenger, and twice the price of a Jaguar XK.*

Right: *Front elevation shows tall 16-inch wheels enveloped gracefully by curved wing-line. Grille is a flattened version of the traditional BMW 'kidneys'.*

Above: *The 507 has brilliant long nose, short tail proportions, spare, muscular and taut. Chassis is shorter by 16 inches than saloon and coupé V8s; body, like the 503, is alloy. Rudge knock-off wheels were a desirable option. 253 507s were built from 1956 to 1959.*

183

Above: *Period cutaway shows torsion bar suspension front and rear, Alfin finned alloy drum brakes (front discs came in late in production) and firmed-up Koni shock absorbers.*

Left: *V8 engine was the hottest available at the time, using twin Zenith carbs for a claimed 150bhp at 5000rpm (some say 160bhp at 5600rpm). It had cooling problems in this sportscar installation and twin carbs could flood, causing underbonnet fires in hot weather. Some American buyers fitted Chevy V8s.*

Above: *Rudge knock-off wheels were an attractive 507 option, though plain hubcaps were standard.*

Above right: *Pop-out door handles were elegant, effective.*

Right: *507 cabin was roomy for a sportscar, and well equipped. Most gauges were carry-overs from other V8 models. All 507s had a floor-shift.*

Opposite page

Top: *507 buyers could also opt for this elegant hardtop, which blended perfectly into the car's overall styling.*

Below: *507s were quick in their day: top speed depended on the axle ratio fitted but at highest estimate was around 137mph, with 0-60mph in about 11 seconds. Steering could not be described as sporting, but the car could cover the miles quickly and comfortably.*

This page

Right: *Period V8 brochure showing 503 and 507.*

Below: *3200 CS was styled by Bertone (where the young Giorgetto Giugiaro was then working) in 1961 and was based on the chassis of the then-ageing 3200S saloon, with the ultimate 160bhp engine. Depth of chassis was hidden brilliantly (note deep sill) and glassy green house provided a foretaste of future CS coupés. Car was fast in a straight line — 124mph — but great weight militated against vigorous acceleration. Bare shells were assembled in Turin and shipped to Munich for completion. Only 603 were built but the car was a styling milestone.*

Left: 3200 CS cabins were plush. Pillarless side windows went down electrically, 503-style dials were mounted in an elegant rosewood dash, and seats were covered with thick leather. Unlike the 503, there was room to lounge in the rear of the CS.

Above and left: One-off 3200 CS cabriolet was built for BMW supremo, Harold Quandt.

Right: Between 1955 and 1962 BMW kept their corporate head above water by selling bubblecars. The Isetta was built under licence from ISO in Italy and used BMW's own 250cc and 300cc air-cooled single-cylinder motorcycle engines. The 600, pictured here, was a grown-up version with four seats, two cylinders and two doors. The car was significant technically, in that it introduced the BMW semi-trailing arm.

Right and below: Designed by Michelotti, the 1959-65 700 was more of a 'real' car, with a 697cc twin in the back and the same (advanced) suspension as the egg-like 600. It was the first BMW to use unitary construction. The coupé appeared first, the two-door saloon developing from it in 1960. Later came the longer wheelbase LS, higher-output Sport and CS versions, and a Baur cabriolet. The 700 was an important lifeline for BMW before the introduction of the 1500 saloon.

New Class, New Beginning
From 1500 Saloon to 2000CS

BMW's postwar success story started with the 1500 'New Class' saloon of 1961, the middle-market car which set engineering trends for the 1960s and 1970s. Highlights were a new overhead cam engine, semi-trailing arm rear suspension and a smart four-door body which remained in production for 10 years. It sired the even more successful two-door cars — 1600-2 and 2002 — and a plush luxury coupé.

The 1500 saloon was announced at the 1961 Frankfurt Show, with production starting in October 1962. With a top speed of 92mph, good roadholding and a supple ride on its new strut/trailing arm suspension, it was among the best 1½-litre family cars in the world.

Right: Engine, by Alexander Von Falkenhausen, was a fine, smooth unit with its single overhead cam, V-formation valves and strong five-bearing bottom end. Free-revving and smooth power was boosted to 80bhp within the first year and by 1963 it had been joined by an 1800 version, including a 110bhp twin-Solex unit. A two-litre block arrived in 1965 and the unit found further fame in the 1968 2002, by which time it had fuel injection too. It lived on until the mid-1980s in the second-generation 3-Series.

Below: The 1500 was joined by the 1800 in 1963. This is the 1800 Ti, with twin Solex carbs and 110bhp. The ultimate 1800 was the Ti/Sa, a 130bhp sold only to licensed racing drivers. 1500 was replaced by the 1600 in 1964.

Above: Most common of the New Class range in the UK is the 1966-1972 2000. The car's lines look heavy now, but were crisp by mid-range saloon standards in the mid-1960s.

Left: The 2000 used oblong tail-light lenses. Boot was huge.

Left: Front end featured distinctive wide-band front lights compared with single round units on 1500, 1600 and 1800.

Right: Cabins on the two-litre cars were smartened up, too, with hooded instrument cluster. Cars came with manual four-speed transmission or three-speed ZF automatic. Both versions were fast, able to top 100mph with strong acceleration.

Below: The four-cylinder engine was given a longer stroke for 1990cc and 100bhp in single Solex form. Later there was a two-carb TI with 120bhp and then the Kugelfischer-injected tii (from 1969) with 130bhp. This was the first production BMW with injection, capable of 115mph. Looks were identical apart from badging.

Below right: Period 2000 sales brochure shot lets the car speak for itself.

BMW 2000

Above: *1965 2000 CS coupé was BMW's new top-of-the-range luxury offering based on the New Class saloon engineering and was the first car to use the two-litre engine.*

Left: *Styled by Wilhelm Hofmeister, the car had strong links with the old 3200 CS which it effectively replaced, though front-end was very different. This example has the British-market twin-light treatment…*

BMW 2000 CS/C Automatic

Left: *…but Continental-spec models, like this automatic, had more dramatic oblong lights, often referred to as 'oriental eyes'.*

Above: *Cars were produced by Karmann in quite small numbers: just under 12,000 were built, mostly manual gearbox versions with the twin-carb 120bhp CS engine. Autos came with 100bhp single-carb lump.*

Right: *Engine provided a creditable 115mph with 0-60mph in 11 seconds, though punch was never considered adequate for the high price of the 2000 CS (in the UK, it cost more than an E-Type). The ride quality was excellent, however, and the cars always had thoroughbred handling with fine brakes. Only 140 were imported into the UK, conversion to rhd being carried out by the British concessionnaires.*

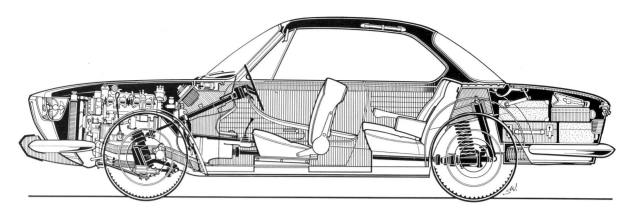

Above: *Cutaway shows how roomy the two-litre coupé was. Seats were thicker than saloon items, and boot was similarly spacious.*

Below: *Cabins were plushly trimmed, with a hand-finished teak dashboard and door cappings and electric windows all round. As with the 3200 CS, the side-windows were pillarless.*

Compact Performance
The 02 Range, from 1600 to Turbo

MORE than any other BMW, the 02 cars established the marque's image for the 1960s and 1970s: quality, performance, handling and comfort, in a machine that was compact and unpretentious. The range spanned 13 separate derivatives over more than a decade of production, from the game little 1600 to the wild Turbo, with estates and convertibles between. They are still a common sight on the road today.

Below: First of the 02 range was the plain 1600-2 of March 1966. Suspension and engines were shared with the four-door New Class cars: the single-carb 1573cc engine, four-speed manual box, disc/drum brakes and strut/railing arm underpinnings. However, in the new two-door body, lighter by 500lbs, performance and handling were even better. Lower price made its own appeal, too, and the car was soon joined by a 1600-2 Ti with twin carbs.

Above: Baur designed this pretty 1600 cabriolet in September 1967: a rare variant, of which only 1,682 were built up to 1971.

Left: The 1600 version of the 02 was dramatically overshadowed when the new two-litre 2002 appeared in 1968. With really gutsy performance — even without twin carbs — the 2002 quickly became BMW's best-selling single model. Top speed was 107mph, with 0-60mph attainable in under 10 seconds. Handling, roadholding and braking remained first class.

Below: Engine was straight out of the 2000 saloon, seen on left with four-speed manual box and installed in the 2002. Cars also came with ZF three-speed automatic, a self-shifter which actually took very little away from the model's excellent acceleration. There was an injected version — the Tii — from 1971 onwards, and briefly a twin-carb version known as the Ti.

Opposite page
Main picture: An early, round tail-light car as built up to 1974.
Insert: A post-74 version featuring new-style bumpers with rubber inserts, sculptured five-inch rim road wheels, square tail-lights and blacked-out front side grilles.

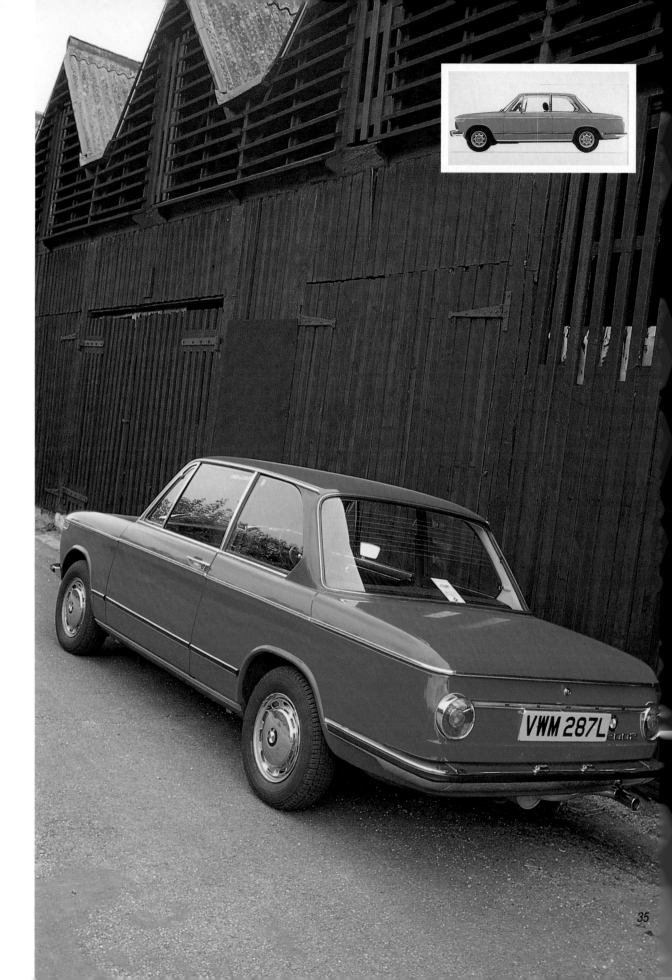

Opposite page
Building the 2002. Over 400,000
were sold between 1968 and 1976.

Left: Early interior shows bleak
use of black plastic almost
everywhere, with big, old-
fashioned, thin-rimmed wheel.

Left and below: Later car had
all-cloth seats, padded wheel and
wood trim around instruments.

36

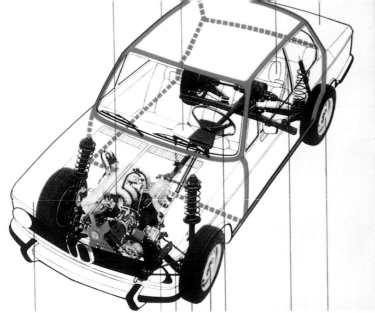

Left:. Cutaway shows classic front engine, rear-drive layout of the 2002, with MacPherson strut suspension, worm and roller steering, disc/drum brakes. This car has the fuel-injected 130bhp Tii engine.

Below: Alpina offered tuning items for the really keen 02 driver, including five-speed box, high-compression head.

Above: Touring three-door estate was BMW's answer to the Reliant Scimitar GTE. It was offered from 1971 to 1974 with 1600, 1800, 2000 and 2000tii engines.

Right: It wasn't the most elegant of estates, despite Michelotti's reshaping of the tail end. The car was more sensitive to side-winds, too.

Right: Still, there was a fair amount of extra load space with the seats folded down, and they split 50/50 as well. Rear shock absorber top mountings intruded on load space.

The bodywork

BMW's principle for the bodywork of a car is compact outside and spacious inside. And the best example for this is the BMW Touring.

The aerodynamic shape of the BMW Touring was created in a wind tunnel. The outstanding features are the slanted windscreen and the "fastback". This makes air resistance decrease, and the top speed increase. It also improves fuel consumption. BMW applies the most modern methods to counteract rust and corrosion. We use the so-called cavity sealing procedure for protecting parts of the bodywork that normally cannot be reached. This new method prevents corrosion before it has even started.

Above: *Brochure shot shows ultimate Tii Touring in garish 'seventies orange, with optional alloy wheels.*
Below: *Baur carbriolet is shown here in later square-light guise, built for just one year. The car came only with the stock 2002 engine. 2,517 were sold.*

Opposite page: *Baur, the Stuttgart coachbuilder, replaced the 1600 cabriolet with the Targa-roofed 2002 in 1971, with removable centre section, fold-down rear portion and integral roll-bar. It was 110lbs heavier than the closed 2002.*

Opposite page and right:
The ultimate performance 2002
was the Turbo, a 130mph hotshot
announced at the Frankfurt Motor
Show in 1973. With its lowered
suspension, fatter tyres, spoilers
front and rear, flared arches and
bold decals, it was a hooligan's
delight — though BMW soon
thought better of the reversed
Turbo script on the front spoiler.
Surprisingly, the car retained rear
drum brakes but gained a larger
fuel tank and could be had with a
five-speed gearbox.

Below: The 2002 Turbo engine
used a KKK turbocharger with
Kugelfischer injection, for an
output of 170bhp at 5800rpm.

Above: In the relatively light 2002 performance was stunning, though power came in so unprogressively that it could catch the unwary. The engine's compression ratio was lowered to avoid detonation.

Left: Last of the 02 range to be introduced was the 'poverty' 1502 of 1975. It actually used the 1573cc engine, but in low-compression 75bhp form. With less chrome trim and a plainer cabin, the car was built for the energy crisis years but was so popular that it outlived the rest of the 02 range. 72,635 were built before production halted in 1977.

Sporting Refinement
From 2500/2800 to 3.0CSL

DESPITE the success of the 'New Class' four-door saloons and the 02 Series, BMW longed to return to the luxury sector, a market they had not competed in since the demise of the big V8 saloons in 1963. They eventually made their luxury car comeback in 1968 with the six-cylinder 2500/2800 saloons — technical big brothers in many respects to the established four-cylinder machines. They were unique in the luxury car market at that time in offering sporting dynamics with big-car refinement. The engine — a brand new in-line SOHC six — was reckoned to be the best in-line six in the world, while the chassis offered sharp handling with a marvellously supple ride. Out of the original 2500/2800 grew the 3.0- and 3.3-litre cars, as well as a range of beautiful CS, CSi and CSL coupés.

Below: The big saloon as it appeared in the autumn of 1968: handsome and unostentatious. This is the 170bhp 2800, with Boge Nivomat self-levelling rear suspension for the semi-trailing arm rear-end, limited slip diff' and 124mph top speed. 2500 saloon looked identical.

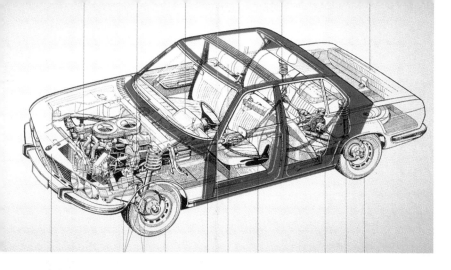

Left: The layout of the big saloons was very similar to that of the established four-cylinders: in-line, overhead cam engine, canted over, driving the rear wheels; four-speed manual/three-speed automatic transmissions; strut/ trailing arm suspension. The six-cylinder cars had the added refinement of all-round disc brakes and power-assisted steering.

Above: The car had a classic BMW face with central kidneys, twin headlights. This is a later mid-1970s example.

Left: Tail showed clean lines, too, with engine-size script on the bootlid. The big saloons were penned by BMW in-house stylist Hofmeister.

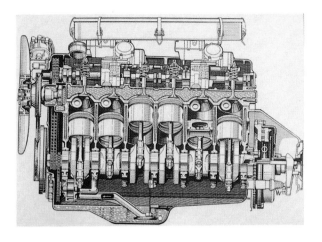

Above: The engine was another Von Falkenhausen jewel: single overhead camshaft, alloy head and triple-hemispherical combustion chambers made it the smoothest and most potent six-cylinder unit around. The 2500 produced 150bhp, the 2800 170bhp, breathing through twin Zenith carbs. It gained injection — Bosch electronic — in the early 1970s and lives on in the 535i, though it will eventually be replaced by BMW's latest three- and four-litre V8s.

Above right: Period brochure promoted power allied with safety. This is the early model with chrome side grilles at the front.

Below: For 1971 the engine was enlarged to three litres, giving 180bhp and 130mph top speed. Most of these cars came with automatic transmission. This is an early 3.0 S on standard steel wheels. Vented rather than solid disc brakes were used all round.

BMW at Dungeness Nuclear Power Station.

The 132mph BMW 3.0Si.
When it's a matter of power.

Power not for its own sake, but for what it can achieve. For those with a natural regard for power look beyond the prestige of ownership and appreciate a BMW for its true value. The BMW 3.0Si provides opportunities to overtake confidently when others must cautiously hold back. Its 220 brake horsepower engine retains latent reserves : in hazardous situations Apollo-like acceleration is readily on hand to speed you clear. The BMW 3.0Si has electronic fuel injection precisely-metered by its own compact computer. With heated rear window, dual circuit braking, fitted headrests all-round and laminated windscreen all fitted as standard equipment. Unlike some luxury three-litres, the BMW 3.0Si isn't an extravagant decoration. It's a powerful Sports Saloon that earns its keep in the nuclear power age.

Unbeatable BMW present a range of Sports Saloons starting at £1899

Prices of the BMW range : 102 mph (Autocar test report) BMW 1602 : £1899 – 113 mph (Autosport) BMW 2002 : £2145 – 106 mph (Motor) BMW 2000 Touring : £2349 – 119 mph (Autosport) BMW 2002tii : £2499 – 121 mph (Autocar) BMW 2500 : £3299 – 127 mph (Autocar) BMW 3.0S : £4030 – 132 mph (Autocar) BMW 3.0Si : £4299 – 125 mph BMW 3.0CSA : £6199. 141 mph BMW 3.0CSi : £6199. ZF Sports Automatic Transmission optional on the BMW 2002 model at £219 and the BMW 2500, and 3.0S models at £269. Prices shown are recommended retail prices including P.T.

Opposite page

Pick of the six-cylinder saloon crop was the 3.0 Si with Bosch electronic fuel injection replacing the twin Zenith carbs. Power went up to 200bhp, economy and smoothness improved, and top speed passed the 130mph mark. With manual transmission — which most cars had — it was among the world's fastest-accelerating four-door saloons.

Above right: *To compete with the long wheelbase Mercedes, BMW devised the 3.3 L in 1974, with 100mm added to the wheelbase to allow more rear passenger space. The longer-stroke 3295cc unit gave 190bhp, came with carbs and automatic transmission as standard. Leather seats and air-conditioning were often fitted. Between 1976 and 1977 there was a slightly shorter-stroke 3210cc variant with injection, called the 3.3 Li. There were long-wheelbase 2.8 and 3.0 versions as well.*

Middle right: *Alpina produced a tuned 250bhp 3.0 Si, boosting top speed to 146mph and reducing 0-60mph time to 6.2 seconds. The car used Kugelfischer rather than Bosch injection, hemi-head combustion chambers with higher compression, heavy-duty clutch and stiffened suspension. Acceleration was equal to a Maserati Bora's, but the conversion cost £2,700 on top of the Si saloon's already high price.*

Right: *First of the six-cylinder coupés was the 2800 CS, introduced at the same time as the saloons in 1968. From A pillar back it used the shell of the old 2000 CS, together with the drums, rear suspension etc. The elegant nose was new, though, and the car sat on handsome alloys as standard. 9,399 were built.*

Above: *3.0 CS of 1971 had the bigger 180bhp engine of the 3.0 S saloon and vented disc brakes all round, but looked identical to the 2800 coupé which it replaced. Production of 3.0 CS coupés reached 11,063 and the car was also available as the 136mph 3.0 CSi (8,199 built) with 200bhp Bosch injection engine. As with the 2000 and 2800 coupés, Karmann built the bodies, but quality control was not all it should have been.*

Left: *Handling of the coupés was excellent, even if not up to the standard set by the saloons which used wider rear track. Power steering was standard.*

Above: The famous CSL Homologation Special started life as this stark German-spec. car: chrome wheelarches hid wider Alpina alloy wheels, side windows were Plexiglass, door, bonnet and bootlid were in aluminium, and the bonnet was held down by quick-release catches. Rear bumper — there was none in front — was made of carbon fibre. Injection or carburettor 3.0-litre engines were used and suspension was stiffened. Built from thinner-gauge steel, the CSL was 400lbs lighter than the CS/CSi.

Above right: UK importers considered the standard item too basic for British tastes. They re-equipped the car with CS bumpers, glass windows and the luxury equipment of the standard car, but kept the alloy panels. Tiger stripes were for the CSL only.

Right: The British CSL was only 140lbs lighter than the CS/CSi and even reverted to standard suspension. 500 of these rhd cars were sold, and for a time they replaced the CSi in the UK market until buyers complained about the difficult-to-get-into bucket seats and dent-prone alloy panels.

Above: *The big BMW's styling is as beautiful today as it was then, displaying perfect balance between roof and body masses.*
Left: *CSL wheels were wider seven-inch items using 195/70 14 Michelin XWX tyres, which explains the chromed arch extensions. Black intake grille is a dummy.*

Opposite page
Bottom: *Even the UK-specification CSL kept the hip-hugging Scheel bucket seats, three-spoke sports steering wheel, sporty black carpets and headlining, sound-proofing, tinted glass and heated rear window. Power window switches were on the centre console around the gearstick; German-spec. lightweights had fixed rear side windows and wind-down front glass.*

Above: As on all the coupés, the CSL's side-windows were pillarless — rear panes do a strange motorised dance before almost disappearing into the side panel and are slow to operate. Structural rigidity was not as good as the saloons'.
Right: 'C' pillar doubled as an interior air outlet.

Above: All British CSLs used the Bosch-injected engine, which in the lightweight had a slight bore increase to give 3003cc — for homologation purposes — though output was unchanged at 200bhp. Performance was identical to that of the CSi and the engine was smooth, free-revving and flexible, with the added bonus of a lovely exhaust note. Autocar managed 133mph on test, and 0-60mph in 7.3 seconds. Handling was crisp but tail-happy in the wet.

Special RHD Equipment for Great Britain.
BMW 3.0 CSL

Left: Brochure for the rhd CSL talks of 'City Package'. The car came in a wild range of lurid orange, red and yellow colours, as well as more subtle shades of silver and gold. It was horribly expensive, its price of £7,399 higher than that of a Jensen Interceptor, six-cylinder Aston Vantage or Porsche Carrera RS.

Above: BMW quoted a 137mph top speed for the 'Batmobile', with 0-60mph in 6.8 seconds. Owners and road test reports of the time confirmed that the spoilers really did work, clamping the back wheels on to the road at speed. The car was available until 1975, with production according to most sources totalling just 39.
Insert: Last of the CSLs was the 3153cc model introduced in August 1973. Mechanically, it had the longer-stroke 3153cc engine, giving 206bhp at 5600rpm. To homologate the BMW's aerodynamic aids for European Touring Car racing, the CSL was given a rubber-edged lip spoiler on the bootlid, rubber air guides on the wings and a front chin spoiler. Racing kit consisted of the massive wing spoiler shown here, with optional air guide on the roof. Bootlid was now steel, but the car kept other alloy panels and used single plate glass side windows. Unlike the usual CSL, the driver's seat backrest was adjustable.

Overleaf
The last of the coupés was the economy 2.5 CS of 1974-75. With its plain disc wheels, wind-down front windows and unassisted steering, it was intended to boost sales of the coupé during the energy crisis years. The 150bhp 2494cc engine still gave 120mph performance. 844 were sold.

BMW 2.5 CS

A new dimension in driving pleasure for the most discerning: BMW 2.5 CS Coupé.

The New Generation

3, 5, 6 and 7 Series

WITH the introduction of the 5-Series in 1972, BMW began their new model designation system, based on 'thirties practice. The 520/520i replaced the old New Class saloons; the 1975 3-Series took over from the 02 cars; the 6-Series replaced the 3.0 coupés in 1976; and the 1977 7-Series replaced the big saloons. It was a clever way of covering the market, and although not all were as standard-setting as their forebears, sales boomed.

Right: Earliest of the 5-Series cars introduced in 1972 looked like this, with flat bonnet and plain, functional four-door styling. Technically, there were few surprises: MacPherson strut with semi-trailing arms suspended the car, providing excellent handling, grip and ride for the time, and the car was slightly longer and wider than the 2000 saloon it replaced. 520 carburetted and 520i injected versions both offered fine performance and surprisingly good economy. In short, the car was a winner, albeit a rather expensive one.

Above: From 1977 the 5-Series had this revised nose with raised centre section to the bonnet.

Below left: The fascia was a new ergonomic high point, with beautifully legible instruments in a well-lit, handsome, functional setting.

Below: A wide variety of engines was used in the early 5-Series: 1800, two-litre (carburettor or injection), 2.5-litre straight six and even the 2.8-litre six — latterly with injection. Shown here is the M60 two-litre 'small six' which took over from the two-litre four in the 5-Series in 1977. It gave a silky 120bhp.

Above: *1981 re-styling of the 5-Series was so subtle that to many people the differences were invisible. The cars now featured a front spoiler and undertray, the rear deck was raised and roof gutters were eliminated. It was more aerodynamic than its predecessor and almost 200lbs lighter.*

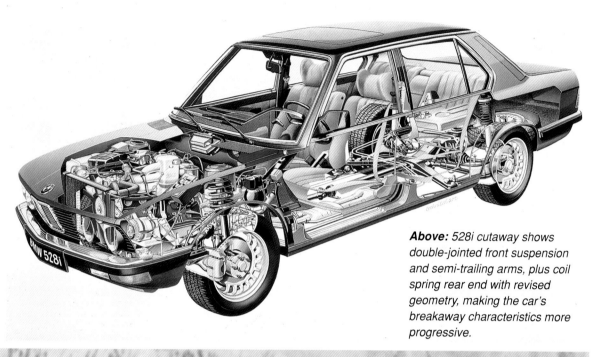

Above: 528i cutaway shows double-jointed front suspension and semi-trailing arms, plus coil spring rear end with revised geometry, making the car's breakaway characteristics more progressive.

The ultimate factory 5-Series was the M5 (also pictured opposite, below) which used the 24-valve, twin-cam BMW Motorsport engine with 285bhp giving 150mph and 0-60mph in 6.5 seconds. The car used advanced engine management, making it as obedient as the single-cam unit. It came with a five-speed sports gearbox as standard, while the chassis featured gas-pressure shock absorbers with progressive action springs at the back. The body was lowered and the M5 sat on fat 220/55 TRX tyres. Braking was by extra-thick vented discs with ABS.

BMW finally replaced the 02-Series cars with the 3-Series in July 1975. A slightly larger and roomier car than its predecessor, the 3-Series retained the classic front engine, rear-drive layout MacPherson strut with semi-trailing arm and coil spring suspension and disc/drum brakes. Steering was now rack and pinion, however, and the four-cylinder engines in the 316 and 318 (which was not available in Britain) were improved by new Solex carburetion.

Below: *Styling was clean and bang up-to-date, but recognisably BMW. This is a 316, capable of 100mph.*

Right: Baur contributed their customary cabrio, with removable Targa roof section. This is the relatively rare 316 variant.

Below: Fastest of the first generation 3-Series cars was the 323i (right), introduced in 1977. With 143bhp from its Bosch-injected in-line small six it was a 120mph car, taking over the mantle of the 2002 Tii. Engines were silky-smooth, but handling could be distinctly tail-happy. There was also a carbureted 320 version, with the same four-light front end. (Car on the left is the MkII version.)

In 1982 BMW revamped the 3-Series, refining the concept rather than radically changing it. Styling was squarer and neater, and improved suspension cured the old cars' oversteer problems. This is the 323i, but there were 316, 318 and 320 versions as well.

Opposite page
Top: A full cabrio version of the 3-Series was another mid-1980s develop- ment. Available with four- and six-cylinder engines, it was pricey but better-looking than the Baur car. It survives into the 1990s until a convertible version of the new 3-Series is available.

This page
Above: Rear suspension gained improved geometry with the coil springs mounted directly on the semi-trailing arms rather than within the struts, with the arm-angle reduced to lessen toe-in. ABS was available on the bigger-engined cars for the first time.
Left: A Baur version of the new 3-Series was briefly offered.
Below: By 1985 there were four-door versions of the 3-Series and a new 2494cc version of the small six with 171bhp allowing 131mph. Both two- and four-door cars suffered from cramped rear passenger space.

Right: The M3 was a 5,000-off Homologation Special for Group A, and a stunningly good driving tool. Using technology gleaned from BMW's experience in Formulas 1 and 2, the engine was a four-valve-per-cylinder in-line four, 2.3-litre with 200bhp. Lowered, with more front castor and gas pressure shock absorbers all round, the M3 provided superb handling with 140mph performance. M3 Evolution of 1989 was an even more exclusive version — only 500 were built — with 20 more bhp, wider wheels and other, more minor changes. Longer gearing countered the increased power: the car was rapid and inspiring, but completely docile. Hard low-speed ride was a small price to pay for such quality.

Top: *There was a convertible M3 for 1989, a resounding £14,000 more expensive than the saloon. It featured chassis strengthening and electric hood, and its power and cornering poise were just as good as the closed car's. Surely a future collectable?*

BMW finally replaced their ageing three-litre coupés in 1976 with the 6-Series — a bigger, heavier coupé, but still elegantly styled. Soft three- and 3.3-litre versions were the initial offerings, but during its 14-year lifespan the car became more rather than less sporting. Last-of-the-line M6 was a four-seater supercar and an assured classic.

Bottom: *The Touring was reintroduced in 1989, though this time around it was to prove more commercially successful. Based on the four-door shell and with the full range of engines, it was really more 'sporting hold-all' than hard-working estate car. Despite being 200lbs heavier than the saloon, performance was good: the 325 version was a 131mph machine. The Touring survives its saloon counterpart, though a new version is on the way.*

Below: *Basic 630 CS with three-litre carburetted engine as it appeared in 1976 — clean and spoilerless. Injected 200bhp 633 looked virtually identical. Strut/trailing arm suspension provided a good ride/handling compromise, though the car would readily oversteer. Power steering was standard, vented disc brakes were used all round. Most cars had three-speed automatic gearboxes, though a four-speed manual was optional. The 628 CSi replaced the 630 in 1979. Stylist of the 6-Series range was Paul Bracq.*

Left: *The 6-Series range was extended in 1978 by the 635CSi, with beefier 218bhp 3.5-litre in-line six and the option of a five-speed manual gearbox. Lowered suspension improved cornering ability (if not roadholding in the wet), while front and rear spoilers, Mahle BBS alloys and striping gave it a slightly 'boy racer' look, reminiscent of the CSL.*

Below: *1983 brought the M635 CSi, with the 24-valve 286bhp twin-cam six. It was one of the world's fastest four-seaters.*

Above: *Based on the 3.5-litre iron block of the established in-line six, the M88 unit — essentially the engine you'll still find in the current M5 — first saw service in the M1. It utilised twin duplex chain-driven camshafts operating four valves per cylinder with a two-piece cylinder head and with separate magnesium castings to carry the cams which ran in seven bearings each. Pent-roofed combustion chambers were used and, rather than the M1's Kugelfischer injection, the M635 and M5 used second-generation Digital Motor Electronics from Bosch (Motronic) for a lusty 286bhp.)*

Above: The property of BMW GB Limited and part of their 'rolling museum', this is one of the last coupés, with de-chromed trim. It cost £9,000 more than the stock 635, but could top 150mph and sprint to 60mph in six seconds while still turning in a very reasonable 20mpg overall fuel consumption. Standard transmission was the ZF five-speeder.

Insert above: There were few visual clues to the cars' twin-cam persona aside from discreet 'M' badging. By the late 1980s the cars had lost the CSi tag. Lower and more firmly sprung than the standard 635, the M handled superbly, though as with any fast rear-drive car its power needed respectful treatment in the wet. Firm low-speed ride was one of the few moans directed at the M635.

Left: Twin-cam six looked handsome under the 6-Series bonnet, gave loads of punch, but made for a smooth, manageable town car.

Above: *Dash changed little in 13 years' production. Later cars had electric seats, though. Note Grippy M-Spec wheel.*
Left: *Rear seat accommodation was generous by coupé standards. All M coupés had leather trim.*
Below: *Wheels were Mahle centre-lock alloys, brakes extra-large vented discs.*

THE 7-SERIES replaced the big three-litre saloons in 1977. Larger and more luxury-orientated than their predecessors, the cars were still sportier than rival Mercedes models. Styling — again by Paul Bracq — was slabby. The series had a 10-year life span and is not yet considered classic — which means that bargains abound.

Below: There were three initial versions of the 7-Series: the carburetted 728 and 730 (with 170 and 184bhp respectively) and the top-line 733 with 197bhp. Four-speed manual and three-speed autoboxes were offered at first, but all models used classic BMW strut front, trailing arm rear suspension with vented disc brakes all round and assisted recirculating ball steering. This early example is pictured in Barcelona.

Left: Inside, 7-Series cars were well-appointed and designed, featuring the driver-orientated wrap-around fascia with check control panel first seen in the 6-Series. The ventilation system was the best-ever in a BMW and rear passengers had generous leg room.

Right: Engine-jiggling in 1979 brought in the 3210cc 732i to replace the 733, a new top-line 735i and injection for the 728.

Below: Most exciting of the 7-Series models was the 745i of 1980. Not a 4.5-litre car, it was in fact the 3.2-litre unit fitted with a KKK turbo for an output of 252bhp. A more economy-conscious alternative to the planned BMW V12 (which would not emerge for another decade), it had a top speed of 140mph with broad-shouldered torque delivery right through the rev range. Engine had a lower compression than other big sixes, but kept the Bosch injection. A collectable big BMW saloon and never produced in rhd form — the steering-column fouled the turbo. The South African 745i used the twin-cam M6 engine. From 1982 — as shown in this picture — the 7-Series had a restyled nose to improve the aerodynamics, revised rear suspension, four-speed lock-up, overdrive ZF transmission and other minor changes. For the British market there was a special 735i SE with all the options. The original 7-Series was replaced in 1986/87 by a new range of big saloons.

Race Car For The Road
The M1

IN essence a homologation special for Group 4 racing, the M1 was BMW's only attempt at making a mid-engined road car. If truth be told, it was not an altogether happy experience: Lamborghini were hired to develop and build the car, but couldn't complete their contractual obligations; BMW pulled out of the deal and the M1 eventually went into production at the Baur works in Stuttgart in 1978, with final assembly by BMW Motorsport who also made most of the chassis components. By the time the car was certified in 1981 it was out of contention, carrying too much weight despite formidable power from its twin-cam six-cylinder engine. A production run of 800 was planned, but only 450 were built. M1s were used in Group 5 and in a Procar series which pitted Formula 1 drivers against privateers in identically prepared cars.

Below: The M1's tubular chassis was built by Marchesi, the fibre-glass panels were hand-formed by Transformazione Italiana Resina, and Ital Design painted the rolling shell. The cars were then shipped to Baur for trimming and suspension and drive train installation. BMW Motorsport carried out final checking and testing.
Insert: Businesslike cockpit of the M1 features 9000rpm tacho, 280kph speedo and leather Recaro seats.

The M1 was styled by Ital Design and isn't reckoned to be one of Giugiaro's more inspired shapes. Though undeniably purposeful in appearance, it seems somehow bland. It certainly lacks the visual drama of Paul Bracq's 1972 BMW Turbo, the 2002 Turbo mid-engined prototype.

Below: The M88 twin-cam 3.5-litre engine — developed from the racing CSL — was mounted longitudinally amidships and drove through a five-speed ZF transaxle. With Bosch-Kugelfischer mechanical injection, it developed 277bhp at 6500rpm.

Above: In terms of performance the M1 was among the world's true supercars, with a top speed of 160mph and a 0-60mph time of six seconds. The car sat on 205/55 tyres and used wishbone and coil spring suspension. The M1 was current from 1979 until 1980, although it was not homologated for Group 4 until 1981.

Below: The 450bhp Group 4 M1. Too much weight compared with Porsche opposition effectively ruled out any chance of success.

The Modern Range

From 3-Series to 8-Series

Below: The new 3-Series was introduced in 1991 in four-door form. Its superb chassis (employing multi-link rear suspension technology from the Z1), its fine four- and six-cylinder engines and its singularly shapely styling gained instant acclaim. 316i, 318i, 320i and 325i versions offered top speeds of 119 to 144mph and up to 35mpg economy with the smallest engines. Insert shows the two-door coupé version, introduced in 1992 with same engine option.

BMWs of the late 1980s and early 1990s are more than ever top-of-their-class machines, staying loyal to traditional rear-wheel-drive engineering, but still further honed and refined. Both 5- and 3-Series models are widely regarded as unrivalled within their categories.

The bigger BMWs have perhaps fared less well. The new V12 engine turned out to be less refined than expected and the big 850i coupé has been branded too clever by half by many pundits, its technical sophistication insulating the driver from the car's responses. The old 'big' six-cylinder — still a top-flight contender despite its years — has been replaced by a pair of new V8s in the 7-Series. The twin-cam 24-valve M5 is perhaps the best BMW of them all — a supercar in everyday clothing.

Above: *M3 version of new E36 3-Series arrived in mid-1992, with a twin-cam three-litre version of the small-six giving 192bhp. Despite excessive weight, the M3 clocked 155mph, achieved a 0-60mph time of six seconds and handled superbly on its unique 17-inch alloys. Styling was subtler than the old M3's, and not by accident, though the car still attracted plenty of attention.*

Below: *Launched in 1993, the convertible version of the new 3-Series featured a roll-over hoop as part of the front screen, strong enough to satisfy US safety laws and support the weight of the 3-Series saloon on top of it. The car's chassis was strengthened to counter scuttle-shake. Blessed with the same excellent handling as the saloon and coupé, the convertible featured a power hood and initially came only with the 2.5-litre in-line six. Car had a good Cd for a convertible of 0.34 and featured a wind deflector to deal with wind buffeting at speed.*

Right: Given the age of the car it replaced, the handsome new 5-Series was one of the most long-awaited BMWs... and no-one was disappointed. From the meekest 520i to the wild M5, its breadth of abilities was unmatched by any of its mid-range saloon rivals. Grip and handling were superb, with neutral cornering poise and none of the old-style BMW oversteer, yet still offering a taut, well-damped ride, almost in the Jaguar class. Cabins, while not over-large, were beautifully arranged. Engines ranged from the two- and 2.5-litre small six (uprated to 24-valve status in 1990) to three- and 3.5-litre versions of the big six, the latter with 141mph top speed and 23mpg economy. All were sweet and smooth and came with slick five-speed manual or four-speed automatic (with a five auto for the small sixes from 1990). Later came a 518i, popular with tax-conscious business users.

Below: The top-of-the-range 5-Series was the M5, with its muscular 315bhp BMW Motorsport 24-valve twin-cam engine. Put together at the rate of 2,000 each year by BMW's Motorsport Division in the suburbs of Munich, its basis was the 535i. The twin-cam engine produced 30bhp more than the old M5, with six percent more torque. The only transmission option was a five-speed manual box. The M5 featured bigger front discs (with ABS), special alloy wheels with turbine blades for extra cooling, and suspension beefed up with thicker anti-roll bars, firmer springs and dampers and self-levelling at the rear. Massive Michelin MXX 235/45 tyres provided outstanding grip and the chassis behaviour set new standards for a saloon car. Top

speed was a resounding 158mph (it would have been 163mph without the 7000rpm rev-limiter); 0-60mph time was 6.4 seconds, and 0-100mph time 15.6 seconds. In all but fourth and fifth gear flexibility, the M5 was more than a match for the 6.3 Aston Martin Virage. The latest 340bhp version with bigger 3795cc engine has improved bottom end flexibility, producing 75 percent of its peak torque at 1800rpm. Top speed is unchanged but 0-60mph is achievable in 5.9 seconds. BMW's Electronic Damper Control (EDC) works on a dashboard switch and controls each wheel individually. The optional Nürburgring package offers rock-hard setting for race-car handling, but is irrelevant on the road.

Left: *Latest addition to the 5-Series line is the Touring Estate. Not a cargo-carrier in the Volvo sense, the Touring is a stylish vehicle with an ingenious split tail-gate: the glass section can be opened separately if need be, or the whole rear door can be lifted in-one for loading larger items. Twin sun-roofs are another neat touch. The 5-series' fine handling qualities remain intact.*

Middle: *In 1986 the new 7-Series arrived, greeted as a big advance on its slab-sided fore-runner. Available as either the 730i (2986cc) or top-of-the-range 735i (3430cc), the cars retained the SOHC in-line six, hitched to five-speed manual transmission or the ZF switchable four-speed auto with sport and economy settings. Expensive but beautifully built, they were refined and comfortable, though only the 3.5-litre car had really impressive performance: 145mph, though still taking a leisurely 9.0 seconds to reach 60mph. Overall fuel consumption was 22mpg. SE versions came with air-conditioning, cruise control and leather seats. All had heated door mirrors and screen washers.*

Left: *The long-awaited BMW V12 engine, on hold since the mid-1970s, made its first appearance in 1987 in the 750iL, 4½ inches longer in wheelbase than the standard 730/735. The 300bhp five-litre unit bestowed super-smooth performance on the big saloon and pushed its top speed to 155mph. Even with the standard four-speed auto, off-the-mark acceleration was brisk, with 0-60mph attained in 7.7 seconds, though thirst was heavy at just 16mpg. The V12 car had wider front grille kidneys to boost prestige — which, at a price well over double that of the standard 730i, it sorely needed.*

Right: The new V12 was a technical tour de force. On 4988cc, it produced exactly 300bhp at 5200rpm and 332lb/ft of torque at 4100rpm. All alloy in construction with single overhead cams per bank, digital motor electronics controlled the ignition and fuelling. It was not all it might have been in terms of refinement and response — delivery was leisurely and unsporting somehow, especially below 2500rpm, and it was not as smooth as Jaguar's V12, then 20 years old. But it was a beautifully presented engine, very symmetrical in layout. At time of writing, a more potent 340bph (but still two-valves-per-cylinder) unit is on the way.

Right: In 1992 BMW introduced their first V8 engine since the 1965 demise of the 3200 CS coupé. Replacing the 735i engine, the new 90-degree engines came in 730i (three-litre 218bhp) and 740i (286bhp) forms and shared nothing with any previous BMW engine. Lightweight units with four cams and four valves per cylinder, they had closed deck cylinder blocks to aid stiffness, plus torsional vibration dampers. Crisp and responsive — not to say throaty by luxury saloon standards — the engines provided beefy performance: embarrassingly, the four-litre unit equalled the big V12 in acceleration, turned in a 150mph top speed, yet gave 10 percent better fuel consumption. The 3.0 unit needed revving to give of its best, but was significantly quicker than the old 735i. Currently the new V8 has yet to appear in other BMWs, though the word is that both 5- and 8-Series cars will eventually use it.

Left: The rear bears a strong resemblance to the 3-Series of 1991, with perhaps a hint of Vauxhall Calibra styling.

Above: For many, the new 850i coupé announced late in 1989 was the most disappointing BMW for a long time. It suffered from technological overkill, its staggering showcase sophistication somehow insulating the driver from the action. It was fast — top speed 155mph — but it somehow failed to feel fast. It handled and gripped the road impeccably, but interested drivers were robbed of involvement by fancy Servotronic steering and ASC traction control. It offered enormous luxury and refinement, yet BMW's V12 could be smoother.

In appearance it was beautiful, combining the classic pillarless BMW coupé greenhouse with a squat, muscular aggression, the M1-style nose and pop-up lights cleaving the air efficiently. Its sheer bulk, and those rather boy racer-ish wheelarch bulges, were its only aesthetic defects.

For the 8-Series it was deemed necessary to develop a totally new rear suspension system, an integral axle with separate links for each wheel; two lower and upper transverse links provide camber control like double wishbones and a single link deals with longitudinal loads. The fifth vertical link joins the longitudinal arm and the upper transverse link with coils and dampers linking the lower arm to the shell. It is so complicated and expensive to build that BMW do not envisage any other production car application.

In conjunction with MacPherson strut front suspension, it endowed the 850 with superbly neutral handling and tremendous grip, but pundits complained of dead, imprecise speed-sensitive Servotronic steering robbing the car of a truly agile feel. The ASC traction control can be switched off to explore the car's high limits. Its fine ride is unfortunately marred by tyre noise. Dampers are electronically adjustable.

Right: Though far from over-stressed, the big BMW V12 has to work at giving the 4000lb 850i truly outstanding performance. It lacks the vitality, response and smoothness expected of a V12, though most would find it impressive enough. In 1993 the 32-valve V8 from the 740 was fitted into the big coupé to make the 840CSi and BMW introduced the 850CSi with the bigger 5.6-litre V12 and six-speed gearbox as standard. Outwardly the cars were all-but identical.

Below: Front bucket seats in 850i are twice as expensive as 750i items; they adjust electrically and have an optional memory facility. With that option comes a steering-wheel which obligingly moves to its highest adjustment to aid exit. The upper belt anchorage is built into the head-restraint arm and automatically adjusts as the seat is moved. Rear seats look good but would not be appreciated by long-legged passengers.

Below: The sweeping dash design was new for BMW, as was the semi-circular rev-counter. Windows drop an inch automatically to aid opening when key is inserted. Thanks to Multiplex electronics, the number of wires in the body was reduced from 23 to just two — a first. Note six-speed manual Getrag gear-change, which has stiffer suspension than the automatic. Some regard this as a marketing ploy, though change is sweet enough. 90 percent of 850s are autos, anyway.

Instant Classic

The Z1

A marriage of traditional sports car with next-generation chassis design (some of which emerged on the new 3-Series), the Z1 was a shortlived open two-seater sportster using 325i saloon running gear devised by 'BMW Technik' in 1986 as a technical showcase. Dramatic drop-down-doors styling gave the car massive poseur appeal, but the Z1 excels as a driver's car: grip and poise are simply superb. Production began at the rate of six cars per day in 1986 and finished in 1991. The Z1 has had no successor and is already highly collectable.

Below: Even if to some the Z1's styling isn't exactly beautiful, it is highly individual and certainly could not be mistaken for anything else. Doors sink into the thick sill electrically when the lock is pressed.

Left: The Z1 stripped of its thermo-plastic body panels. Steel mono-coque chassis was stiff, thanks to zinc filling between welds, thick sills and bracing in scuttle/screen and rear cross-panel. There was virtually no scuttle-shake. Composite fibre sandwich under floor added further to rigidity, providing smooth aerodynamic airflow and excellent corrosion resistance.

Above: The Z1 was the first car to use vertical body parts made of injection-cast thermoplastic, which avoided panel rippling. Note concave bonnet centre. Panels could be removed in 30 minutes — there was talk of offering optional body panels for weekend colour changes! General fit and finish were superb.

Right: Though not wildly fast with its 325i 170bhp engine, the Z1's handling was spectacularly good. Grip was outstanding, thanks to the new 'Z axle' double-wishbone rear suspension which induced toe-in up to 0.65g and toe-out thereafter. The car maintained its go-where-you-point-it poise up to very high cornering speeds; almost nothing could touch it. On dry roads it was impossible to make the tail break away, while on public roads its limits were unfindable.

Left: The Z1's cabin matched the high standards of the rest of the car: clear instrumentation, good driving position and comfortable (if unusual) marble-flecked leather seats. Standard equipment included power windows and mirrors and central locking.

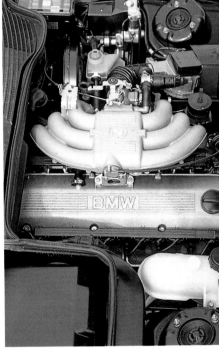

Above: Injected 2.5-litre 325i engine was no match for the car's stunning chassis, though it provided good performance by normal standards: 139mph top, 0-60mph in 7.9 seconds, with sparkling delivery and characteristic smoothness. 24mpg wasn't bad, either.

Left: Beautiful alloy wheels also came as standard.

IN 1966 BMW acquired the assets of Hans Glas GmbH of Dingolfing, with the express intention of using their manufacturing space to expand BMW car production. The Glas range of cars (which had begun with the Goggomobil in the mid-1950s) was gradually phased out, but not before some interesting hybrids had been produced...

Glas Cars

Above: *Glas entered the grown-up car market with the Frua-styled saloon in 1963. Introduced with a 1.5-litre engine, it was enlarged to 1682cc when the car went into production in September 1964.*

Right: *Focus of technical interest was the 80bhp four-cylinder engine with belt drive for its overhead camshaft. Glas had pioneered this feature, now used by virtually every major manufacturer, on the little 1004 saloon in 1962.*

Left: *Conventionally engineered in all other respects, the car was a close competitor of BMW's New Class saloons. When BMW stopped production in 1967, the body presses were shipped to South Africa where the car was sold as the BMW-engined 1804.*

Left and below: *At the 1963 Frankfurt Show, Glas introduced the 1300GT, with a pretty Frua-designed (and built) coupé body and a twin-carb version of the 1304 TS engine giving 75bhp. Later came the 115mph 1700 GT with 100bhp. These cars were nicely-built, fast and nimble.*

Above: When BMW acquired Glas in 1966, they kept on the 1700 GT but equipped it with their own 1600 Ti engine and semi-trailing arm suspension. 1,255 BMW 1600 GTs were built before the plug was pulled in 1968.

Right and below: The ultimate Glas was the 2.6 V8, a Frua-bodied GT car with a 150bhp V8 engine with toothed belt cam drive and a De Dion rear axle. Nick-named 'Glaserati' because of its similarity to a certain Italian super-car, from 1967 it was known as the BMW-Glas 3000GT with a slight (5mm) bore increase and 160bhp. Both versions are rare and desirable.

MUNICH LEGENDS

SALES

Exciting BMW's for those who know more about understeer and oversteer than hands-free dialling and on-board computers...and all cars are inspected by BMW trained engineers to ensure no nasty post-purchase surprises. Buy with confidence... whatever the model.

SPARES

Everything you need to care for your Coupe from the leading 3.0 CS specialists... now offering the same enthusiastic support to owners of all classic and performance BMW's. Call (0892) 852888 - the only part number you need to know.

SERVICE

Full workshop support from a service to a complete mechanical rebuild including performance modifications for road or track, all carried out by BMW trained technicians who never forget... only your satisfaction guarantees our success.

SUPPORT

Restoring a classic 3.0 Coupe or searching for a late model M6? Whatever your interest in the Munich Marque, we're here to help... with experience and enthusiasm that combine to provide a standard of service you can trust.

THE BMW 3.0 CS COUPE CENTRE
The Independent BMW Specialist
Munich Legends, Moons Yard, Rotherfield, Crowborough, East Sussex TN6 3LG
TEL: 0892 852888 FAX: 0892 852417

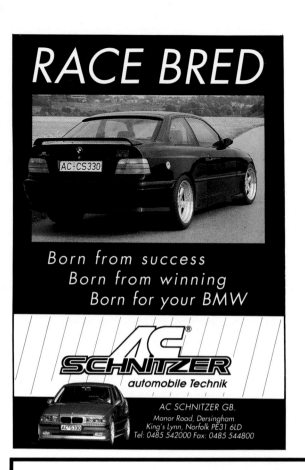

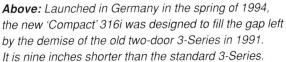

Martin Buckley *has been on the editorial staff of* Classic & Sportscar *magazine since 1988. His work has also been published in* Restoring Classic Cars, Practical Classics, Your Classic, Autoclassic *and* Autocar & Motor. *A two-time BMW owner (2000 CS and 3.0 S saloon), he is the author of* BMW: The Classic Six-Cylinder Coupés, Classics In Colour: Jaguar XJ-Series *and two books in the* Classic & Sportscar 'File' *series on MG and Jaguar E-Type. A book on the Jaguar MkII is currently in preparation. Aged 27, Martin Buckley lives in north London.*

James Mann *holds the enviable position of staff photographer for* Classic & Sportscar *and its sister magazine* Your Classic. *His pictures also appear in* Autosport *and* Autocar & Motor. *A confirmed classic car fan, he has raced and rallied such diverse cars as a Rover 2000 and an MG Midget which he is currently restoring. This is his second book in collaboration with Martin Buckley and a third, on the Jaguar MkII, is well under way. All photographs were taken on Fujichrome film, using a Nikon F4 and a Mamiya RB67. James Mann is 30 and lives in south London.*